Canadian Curriculum

Science Smart

Grade 3

Credits

Photos (Cover "girl looking at grass" Sergiy Bykhunenko/123RF.com, "girl blowing windmill" Logos/123RF.com, "bee" szefei/123RF.com, "lorikeets" Tyler Panian/123RF.com)

Printed in China

ISBN: 978-1-927042-85-4

Contents

ISBN: 978-1-927042-85-4

Grade 3

ISBN: 978-1-927042-85-4

ISBN: 978-1-927042-85-4

Plants

In this unit, students will:

- identify the major parts of plants and understand their functions.
- identify the two different types of trees and their characteristics.
- understand what plants need for growth.

ISBN: 978-1-927042-85-4

1

A. **Label each part of the plant with the given words. Then colour the plant as specified.**

flower leaf root stem

Colour the flowers yellow, the leaves green, and the stem and the roots brown.

ISBN: 978-1-927042-85-4

B. **Read each riddle and write what it is about. Write "roots", "stem", "leaf", or "flower". Then draw a picture to go with it.**

1. This part of the plant
   Holds it up to the sun
   Inside is a place
   For water to run

   ____

2. Make food from sunshine
   Air in and air out
   This part of the plant
   Is hard-working, no doubt

   ____

3. They search for water
   They grow underground
   With them in place
   The plant can't move around

   ____

4. This is the part
   That forms the seed
   If there's going to be new plants
   That's just what they need

   ____

ISBN: 978-1-927042-85-4

1

C. **Fill in the blanks. Then identify the trees. Write "conifer" or "broadleaf" beside each tree.**

broadleaf	conifer	evergreen	fall
flowers	leaves	needle-like	

1. There are two types of trees: ____________ and ____________ trees.

2. Broadleaf trees typically lose their ____________ after changing colour in the ____________ . They also produce ____________ although they are not easy to see.

3. Conifers have ____________ leaves and produce seed cones. They are usually ____________ .

____

____

____

____

ISBN: 978-1-927042-85-4

D. **Look at each plant and find the thing it needs. Write the answer on the line.**

Science Corner

Most plants need sunlight, air, and water to live and grow.

1. 

Although I have water and air, I need ______________ as well.

2. 

Has:
water, sunlight

Doesn't have:

____

3. 

Has:
air, sunlight

Doesn't have:

____

E. **Put each item from the list in the store where you will find it. If something can be found in both stores, put it where the circles overlap.**

- tomato
- fern
- parsley
- onion
- peach
- tulip
- broccoli
- celery
- ivy
- spruce

ISBN: 978-1-927042-85-4

1

Try this!

Plants in Your House

Take a walk through your house to find things that are from plants. Then make a chart to show how we use plants.

Plants breathe in air and give us oxygen. Plants give us food, provide shade, and much more. They give us lots of things, like seeds for food, wood for our homes and furniture, and fibres for clothing and blankets.

	Things	We use them for
e.g.	chair	furniture

Checklist

Are you able to...

- ☐ identify the major parts of plants and understand their functions?
- ☐ identify the two different types of trees and their characteristics?
- ☐ tell what plants need for growth?

ISBN: 978-1-927042-85-4

More about Plants

2

In this unit, students will:

- learn the life cycle of a bean plant.
- understand the effects of the seasons on plants.
- identify the major parts of a tree and their functions.
- identify the major parts of a flower and their functions.
- show the development of a fruit.

ISBN: 978-1-927042-85-4

2

A. **Draw a path to show the growth of a bean plant.**

B. **Look at the pictures of a cherry tree in four different seasons. Write which season the tree is in.**

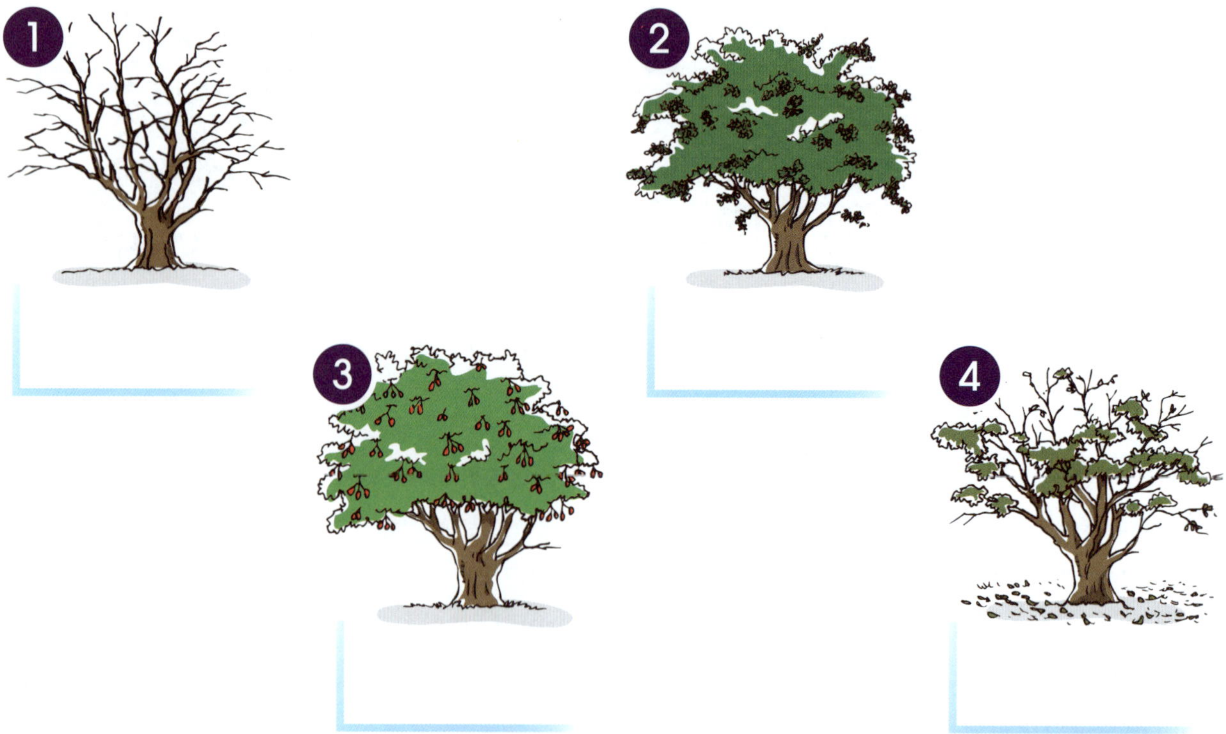

 ISBN: 978-1-927042-85-4

C. Draw lines to label the parts of the tree. Then fill in the blanks with the given words.

1.

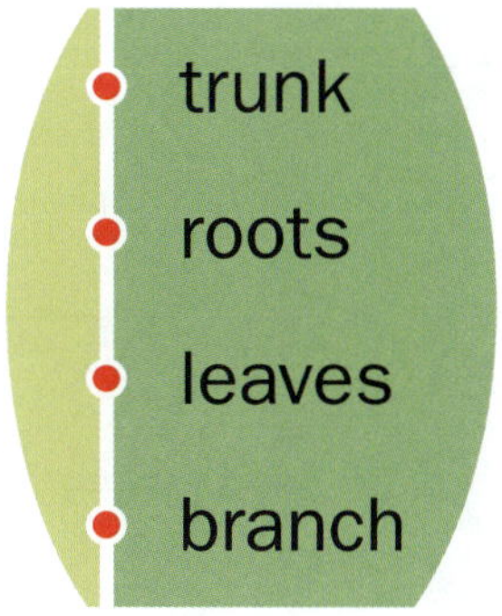

branches bark leaves plants nutrients water trunk

Trees are the largest 2. ________________ in the world. Instead of a stem, trees have a 3. ________________ to support the 4. ________________ . It also delivers 5. ________________ and 6. ________________ to the 7. ________________ of the tree. This part of the tree is protected by a special skin called 8. ________________ .

Unlike animals, plants keep growing throughout their whole life.

ISBN: 978-1-927042-85-4

2

D. Match each part of a flower with the correct description. Fill in the missing letters.

ovary sepal petal pistil stamen

1. __t__ __ __ __ •
2. __ __p__ __ •
3. __ __s__ __ __ •
4. __v__ __ __ •
5. __ __t__ __ •

- usually green, protects the bud until the flower opens
- pollen producing, it has a tall thin stalk
- the centre stalk of a flower that houses the ovary
- coloured leaf-like part of a flower that attracts insects and other pollinators
- ball-shaped part at the base of the pistil where seeds develop

 ISBN: 978-1-927042-85-4

E. **Label the parts of the flower with the given words on the previous page. Then circle and colour the correct parts of the flowers.**

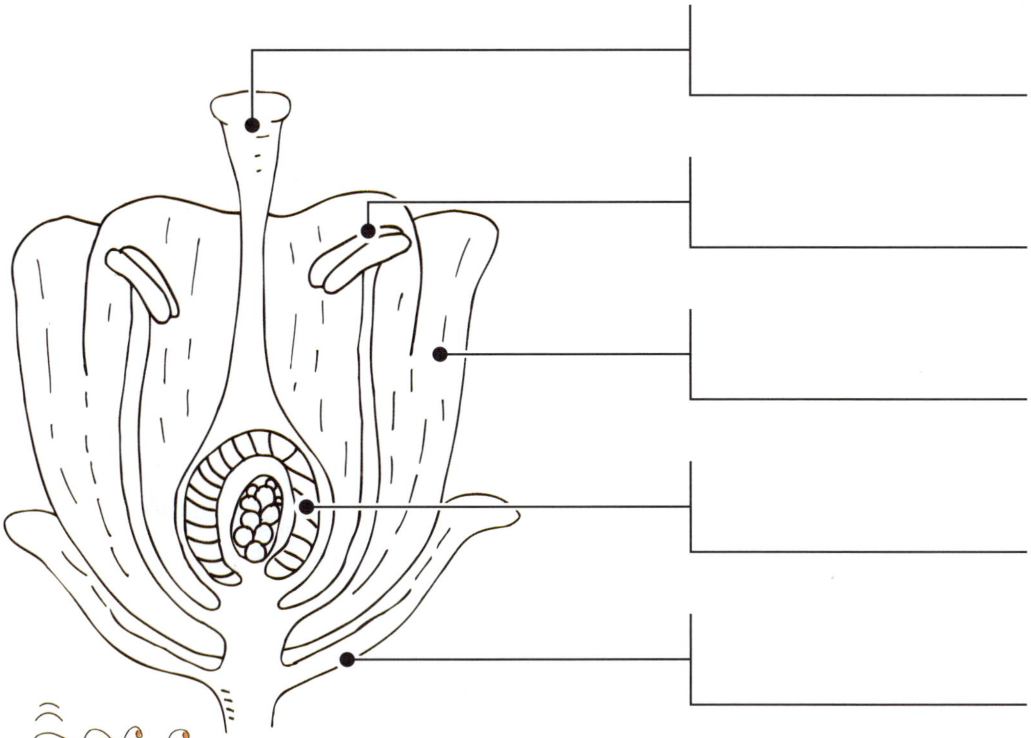

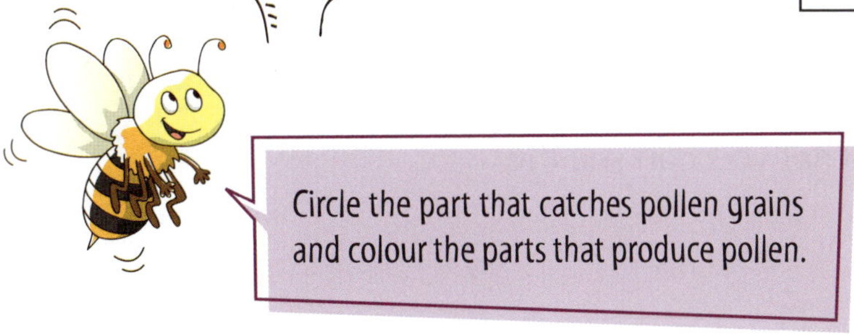

F. **Put the pictures in order to show the process of the formation of a fruit. Write 1 to 4.**

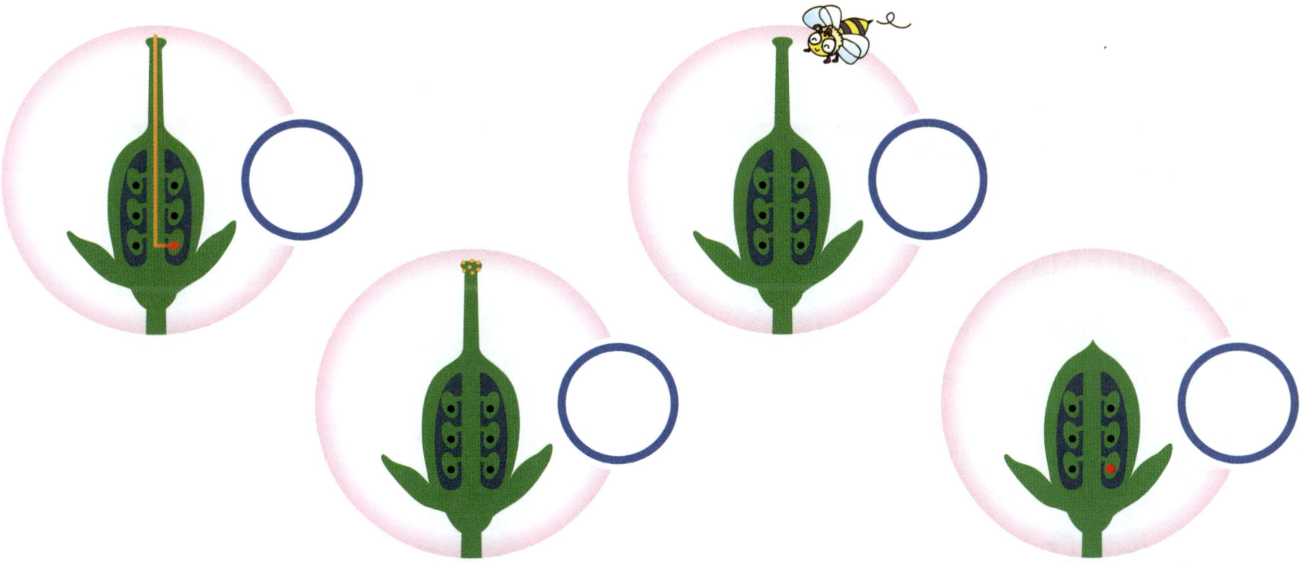

ISBN: 978-1-927042-85-4

2

Try this!

Water Movement in Plants

Materials:

- a celery stick with some leaves
- red food colouring

Science Corner

Plants transport minerals and water up from the roots to the leaves through tubes called xylem.

Steps:

To prove that water travels up the stem to the leaves, you can fill your pail with water. Then place a bunch of celery in the pail and cut a stick with some leaves still attached in the water. Let the stick stay in the pail and take out the bunch of celery. Put some food colouring in the pail. Let the stick sit in the water overnight. Write what you can see the next morning.

____

____

____

____

Checklist

Are you able to...

- ☐ tell the life cycle of a bean plant?
- ☐ show the effects of the seasons on plants?
- ☐ identify the major parts of a tree and their functions?
- ☐ identify the major parts of a flower and their functions?
- ☐ show the development of a fruit?

ISBN: 978-1-927042-85-4

Magnets

3

In this unit, students will:

- learn what magnets are and understand that the Earth is a huge magnet.
- recognize the poles on a magnet and their properties.
- understand how magnets repel or attract each other.

ISBN: 978-1-927042-85-4

3

A. Fill in the blanks with the given words.

north
magnet
south
magnetite
whales
nickel

Science Corner

Magnets are naturally found in a rock called magnetite. Sometimes it is called lodestone. We don't usually see them in that form, though.

1. The end of the magnet that points to the north is called the ____________ pole; the end that points to the south is called the ____________ pole.

2. The rock ____________ is a natural magnet formed deep in the Earth over thousands of years.

3. The Earth's core is made mostly of iron and ____________ . This core makes the Earth act like a huge ____________ .

4.

Scientists believe that some ____________ use the Earth's magnetic lines of force to find their way in the ocean.

ISBN: 978-1-927042-85-4

B. Read what Sally says. Help her draw a magnet in the space provided. Label its north pole and south pole. Then use arrows to point at the parts with the strongest magnetic force.

> A magnet's force is strongest at its poles, that is, at either end of the magnet. Every magnet has a north pole and a south pole.

C. Fill in the blanks to describe the pictures.

different south north like

1\.

The __________ pole of a magnet pulls on, or attracts, the north pole of another magnet. __________ poles attract.

2\.

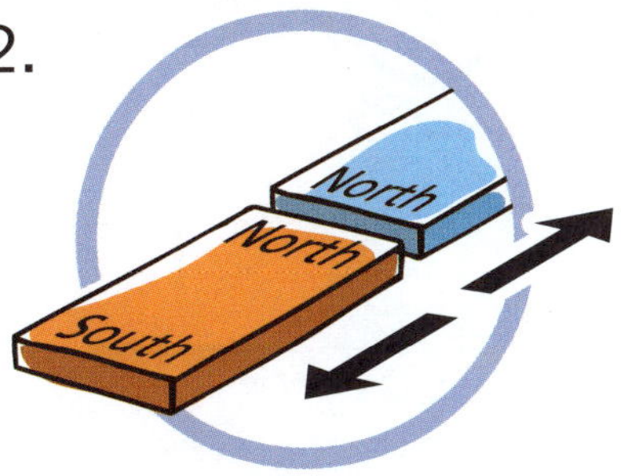

The __________ pole of a magnet pushes away from, or repels, the north pole of another magnet. __________ poles repel.

ISBN: 978-1-927042-85-4

3

D. Tell whether each pair of magnets is going to attract or repel. Write "attract" or "repel" in the boxes.

1.

2.

3.

4.

E. How do we make a triangle with three bar magnets? Write "N" for north and "S" for south to show the poles of the magnets.

1.

2.

ISBN: 978-1-927042-85-4

F. The children are talking about magnets. Guess what they are describing. Write the answers on the lines.

1.

It's the name of a rock that has magnetic properties.

____

This end of a magnet is attracted to the south pole of another magnet.

____

2.

This metal can be magnetic, or even a magnet.

____

It's the way two like poles behave when brought together.

____

3.

It's the way a north and a south poles behave when brought together.

____

ISBN: 978-1-927042-85-4

3

Try this!

How Strong Is Your Magnet?

Materials:

- several different kinds of magnets
- about 20 metal paper clips

Some magnets are stronger than others, and the magnetic force is always strongest at the poles.

Steps:

1. Label the magnets. Pick up one paper clip with one of the magnets. Then put a second paper clip near the first one. Keep adding paper clips until no more paper clips can be held.

2. Try the same experiment with each magnet. Make a chart to record the results. Compare the results to find the strongest magnet.

Magnet					
No. of (paper clips) it holds					

Checklist

Are you able to...

- [ ] tell what magnets are and understand that the Earth is a huge magnet?
- [ ] recognize the poles on a magnet and their properties?
- [ ] describe how magnets repel or attract each other?

ISBN: 978-1-927042-85-4

More about Magnets

4

In this unit, students will:

- know how we use magnets in our daily lives.
- identify the things that make use of magnetic forces.
- identify the magnetic objects.
- learn how movement changes with different magnets.

ISBN: 978-1-927042-85-4

4

A. **Where are the magnets around us? What are the magnets for? Write the correct ending for each verse.**

1. A cupboard, a fridge
   A cabinet and more
   They all use a magnet
   To help close the ______________ .

2. The mountains! The forests!
   To the seas go forth!
   You will not get lost
   With a magnet pointing ______________ .

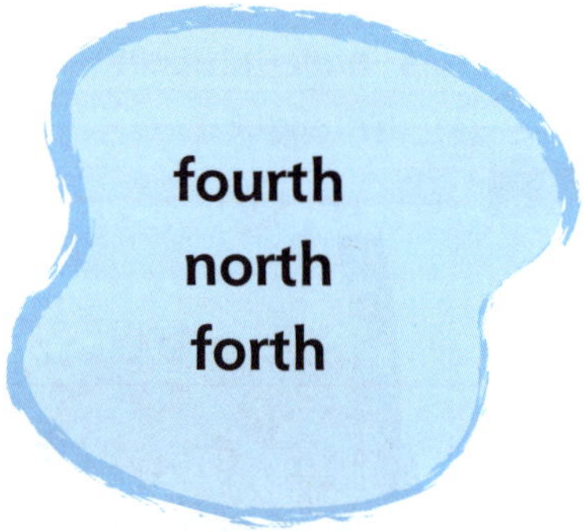

3. Holding things up
   Can be quite a trick
   No nails? No glue?
   Use a magnet to ______________ .

4. I.D. cards, credit cards
   Bank cards to swipe
   They have information
   On their magnetic ______________ .

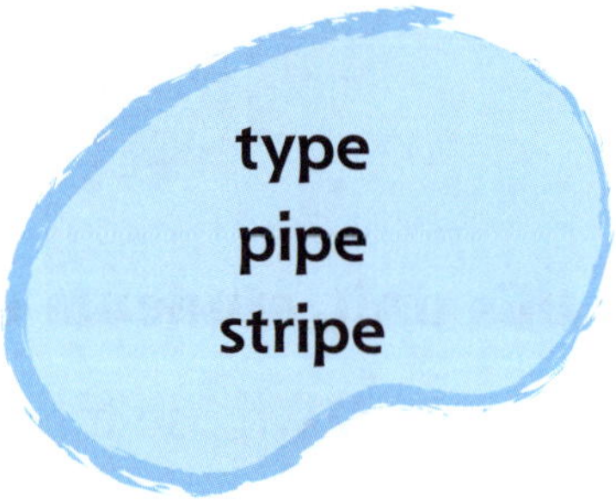

ISBN: 978-1-927042-85-4

B. **Look at the pictures. Check ✔ the things that make use of magnetic forces.**

1.

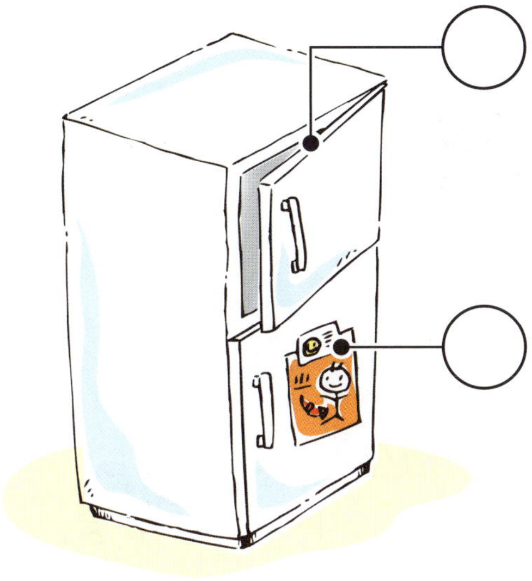

2.

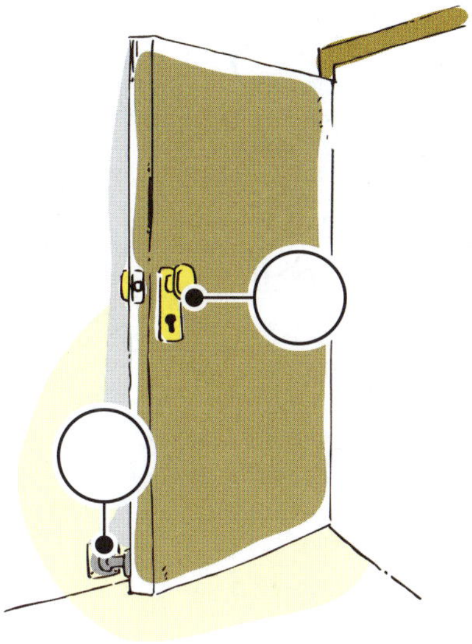

3.

4.

5.

ISBN: 978-1-927042-85-4

4

C. **Draw a line to show the path that the magnet takes to get all the magnetic objects on its way home.**

ISBN: 978-1-927042-85-4

D. Tim has taped a magnet on his toy car. See what experiments he is doing. Help him record the observations.

Experiment 1

1. Tim moves a magnet slowly to the magnet on the toy car. How will the toy car move?

   ____

2. If Tim moves the magnet faster, how will the toy car move?

   ____

3. If Tim uses a bigger magnet and moves slowly to the magnet on the toy car, how will the toy car move (compared to the result in question 1)?

   ____

Experiment 2

4. I move the magnet in my left hand slowly toward the magnet on the toy car. What will happen?

   ____

   ____

ISBN: 978-1-927042-85-4

4

Try this!

Magnetic Objects

Materials:

- a strong magnet
- a paper or plastic box
- a string

Steps:

You need to put something small in the box, such as a screw, a nail, and an eraser. Hang the magnet with a string. Then try to "catch" the things in the box. Make a chart to record the findings.

Things Caught	Things Not Caught

What is common about everything you "caught"?

____

Checklist

Are you able to…

- [ ] tell how we use magnets in our daily lives?
- [ ] identify the things that make use of magnetic forces?
- [ ] identify the magnetic objects?
- [ ] describe how movement changes with different magnets?

ISBN: 978-1-927042-85-4

Forces and Movement (1)

In this unit, students will:

- identify a force as a push or pull by one body on another.
- identify the existence of gravity.
- learn the definitions of different kinds of forces.
- identify the examples of different kinds of forces and tell whether the motions are caused directly or indirectly.

ISBN: 978-1-927042-85-4

5

A. **Look at each picture. Tell whether the force involved is of a push or pull type. Write "push" or "pull" on the line.**

1.

____

A force is a push or pull of an object upon something else. You cannot see forces, but you can see what they do!

2.

____

3.

____

4.

____

5.

____

ISBN: 978-1-927042-85-4

B. Some of the pictures below show the existence of gravity. Find and colour them.

1.

2.

3.

4.

5.

Science Corner

You are a little bit taller when you are lying down. Gravity pulls you down enough to lose that height when you stand up.

ISBN: 978-1-927042-85-4

5

C. Read the definitions of different kinds of forces. Fill in the blanks to complete the names of the forces.

Buoyancy	Friction	Gravity
Magnetic	Muscular	Electrostatic

1. ____________________ Force:

   Attached to bones, muscles pull and allow for movement.

2. ____________________ Force:

   Different charged objects pull toward each other; like charged objects push away.

3. The Force of ____________________ :

   When objects rub against each other, this force works against the movement.

4. ____________________ Force:

   This force sometimes pulls and sometimes pushes.

5. ____________________ :

   Water pushes on you and makes you float.

6. The Force of ____________________ :

   This is the pulling force that the very large Earth has on the very small you. You stick to the planet because of this!

ISBN: 978-1-927042-85-4

D. **Label the pictures with the correct forces on the previous page. Then tell whether the motions are caused "indirectly" or "directly".**

1. ____________________ ;

____

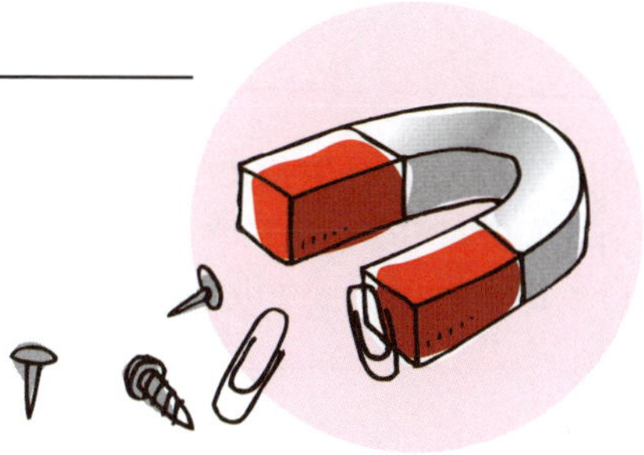

2. ____________________ ;

____

3. ____________________ ;

____

4. ____________________ ;

____

5. ____________________ ;

____

6. ____________________ ;

____

ISBN: 978-1-927042-85-4

5

Try this!

Experiment with Gravity

Materials:

- a coin
- a pencil
- a pebble
- a step stool

Stand on the stool, hold any two of the objects and drop them at the same time from the same height above the ground. Predict and record the results.

Reached the ground first			

Does gravity pull at them equally, regardless of their masses?

____

If you use a piece of paper or a leaf, another force called air resistance will affect the results of your experiment. Crumple the paper up before you drop it. You will find that the result will not be the same.

Checklist

Are you able to...

- ☐ identify a force as a push or pull by one body on another?
- ☐ identify the existence of gravity?
- ☐ define the different kinds of forces?
- ☐ give examples of different kinds of forces and tell whether the motions are caused directly or indirectly?

ISBN: 978-1-927042-85-4

A. Complete the crossword puzzle.

a rock that is a natural magnet

one of the two types of trees

________ force

Like poles ________ .

________ poles attract.

one of the things that plants need

broadleaf different magnetic
magnetite petal repel water

ISBN: 978-1-927042-85-4

B. Check ✔ the correct answers.

1. The cherry tree in spring:

2. The name of the circled part:

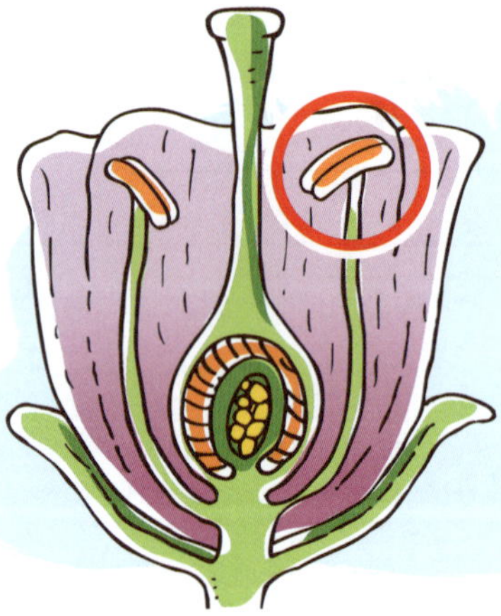

A petal

B stamen

C pistil

D ovary

3. The pictures that show the existence of gravity:

A

B

C

D

ISBN: 978-1-927042-85-4

4. The magnetic objects:

5. The correct diagrams that show the properties of magnets:

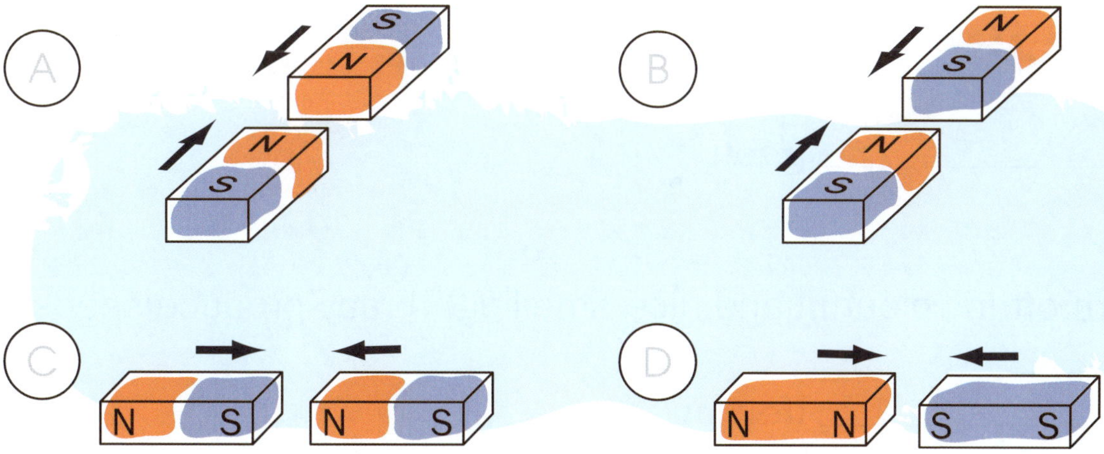

6. The conifers:

ISBN: 978-1-927042-85-4

C. Most plants have the same plant parts. Use the clues to help unscramble the names of these plant parts.

1. I am like a straw. Water travels through me to reach the leaves.

    ________________ (**semt**)

2. We gather water and nutrients from the soil, and we hold the plant in place.

    ________________ (**rstoo**)

3. I am usually green, and I use sunlight and water to make food for the plant.

    ________________ (**fael**)

4. I am often colourful and nice smelling. I may produce seeds.

    ________________ (**lewfor**)

5. I may grow into a new plant.

    ________________ (**dese**)

ISBN: 978-1-927042-85-4

Forces and Movement (2)

6

In this unit, students will:

- understand the meanings of balanced and unbalanced forces.
- show the direction of movement of an object caused by a force.
- understand that the speed or direction of an object will be changed if there is an outside force.
- identify devices that are controlled automatically, at a distance, or by hand.

ISBN: 978-1-927042-85-4

6

A. Look at the pictures. Complete the sentences and label the pictures with the given words.

balanced unbalanced

Science Corner

Forces happen in pairs. When they are unbalanced, there is movement.

1.

Kevin is not moving. The force of gravity equals the force of buoyancy. These forces are ____________ .

2.

The pebble is moving toward the bottom of the lake. The force of gravity is greater than the force of buoyancy. The forces are ____________ .

3.

____

4.

____

ISBN: 978-1-927042-85-4

B. **Using the title of each picture as a hint, decide what movement is shown. Then draw an arrow to show the direction of movement.**

1.

Science Corner

Unbalanced forces cause movement because forces have directions. When we want to show the direction of a force, we use an arrow.

2.

3.

4.

5.

ISBN: 978-1-927042-85-4

C. Look at each picture. Predict the next scene with the new force added. Check ✓ the correct sentence.

1. If the batter hits the baseball with his bat,

(A) the speed and the direction of the baseball will be changed.

(B) the ball will travel in the same direction at a new speed.

2. When the parachutist jumps and opens his parachute,

(A) the parachute will help the parachutist fall at a higher speed.

(B) the parachute will help the parachutist fall at a lower speed.

3. When the car is approaching a stop sign, the driver will step on the brake. Then...

(A) the car will slow down until it stops.

(B) the car will travel at a higher speed.

 ISBN: 978-1-927042-85-4

D. Look at the pictures. Identify the devices that are controlled "automatically", "at a distance", or "by hand".

1.

2.

3.

4.

5.

6.

ISBN: 978-1-927042-85-4

6

Try this!

A Moving Shopping Cart

A force can set an object in motion. It can also make a moving object speed up, slow down, stop, or change its direction. When you go grocery shopping with your parents, you can see how a shopping cart moves when you exert forces on it. But remember, when you do this experiment, make sure you are in a big enough space.

The cart is going forward.

1. How can you make it move faster?

   ____

2. How can you stop it?

   ____

3. You keep pushing the cart, but one of your hands exerts a greater force. What will happen?

   ____

Checklist

Are you able to…

- [ ] explain balanced and unbalanced forces?
- [ ] show the direction of movement of an object caused by a force?
- [ ] show that the speed or direction of an object will be changed if there is an outside force?
- [ ] identify devices that are controlled automatically, at a distance, or by hand?

ISBN: 978-1-927042-85-4

Stability (1)

7

In this unit, students will:

- identify "human-made" and "non-human-made" structures.
- understand the concept of stability in different structures.
- identify the stable and unstable structures in our daily lives.
- predict which body positions provide the most stability.

ISBN: 978-1-927042-85-4

7

A. **Name each structure. Then tell whether each structure is "human-made" or "non-human-made".**

1.

________________ ; ________________

2.

________________ ;

____

3.

________________ ; ________________

4.

________________ ; ________________

5.

________________ ;

____

6.

________________ ; ________________

ISBN: 978-1-927042-85-4

B. Match the facts with the structures on the previous page. Write the names of the structures on the lines.

1. Some are cup-shaped to keep things from rolling around too much.

____

2. It is a free-standing structure supported by a base with a diameter of about 70 m.

____

3. It is a mass structure with a frame structure inside to house the generators.

____

4. Together with mud and stones, the lodge can last for many years.

____

5. A strand of this is stronger than steel of the same diameter.

____

6. This massive structure is entirely made of white marble and its pure white walls are decorated with exquisite stone inlay work.

____

ISBN: 978-1-927042-85-4

7

C. Are the structures stable? Label each as either "stable" or "unstable".

Science Corner

Stability is important in our lives. Things are stable if they stay the way they are meant to be when forces act upon them.

1.

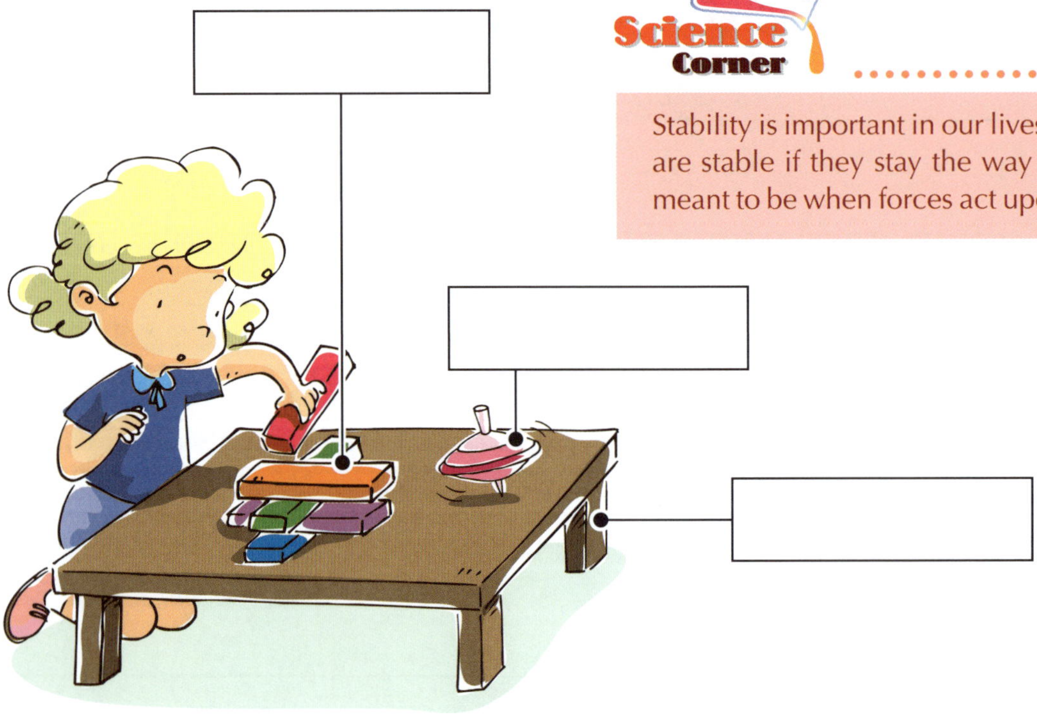

2.

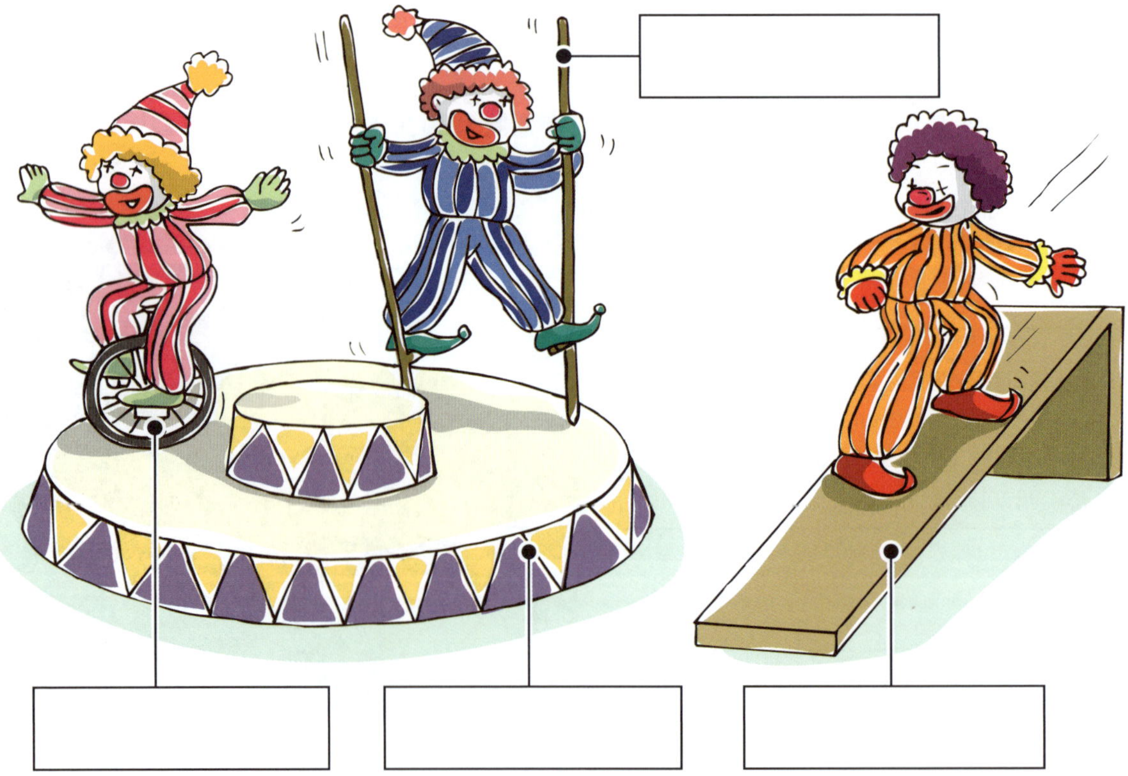

ISBN: 978-1-927042-85-4

D. Predict which body position provides the most stability in each group of pictures. Put the positions in order and write the letters. Then answer the question.

1.

Most stability → Least stability: ____________

Which position do you think I can maintain the longest time?

____

2.

Most stability → Least stability: ____________

Which position do you think I will maintain the shortest time?

____

ISBN: 978-1-927042-85-4

7

Try this!

Forces in Action

You can try this experiment with your friend.

Steps:

1. Stand with your back and heels up against a wall.
2. Have someone place a coin (or some other small objects) in front of you on the floor.
3. Now, without bending your knees, bend down and pick it up.

What happens?

____

____

____

____

You would have difficulty because when you bend over to pick up the object, your centre of gravity shifts, and you lose your stability. Normally, when you bend to pick up something, your hips maintain the centre of gravity to keep you stable.

Checklist

Are you able to...

- ☐ identify "human-made" and "non-human-made" structures?
- ☐ explain the concept of stability in different structures?
- ☐ identify the stable and unstable structures in our daily lives?
- ☐ predict which body positions provide the most stability?

ISBN: 978-1-927042-85-4

Stability (2)

8

In this unit, students will:

- learn different words to describe the effects of the forces at work.
- identify the struts and ties in structures.
- use different ways to increase the stability of structures.
- fix the structures by different ways.

ISBN: 978-1-927042-85-4

8

A. We have different words for actions that involve forces. Write the effects of the forces at work.

bend slide squeeze stretch twist

1.

____

2.

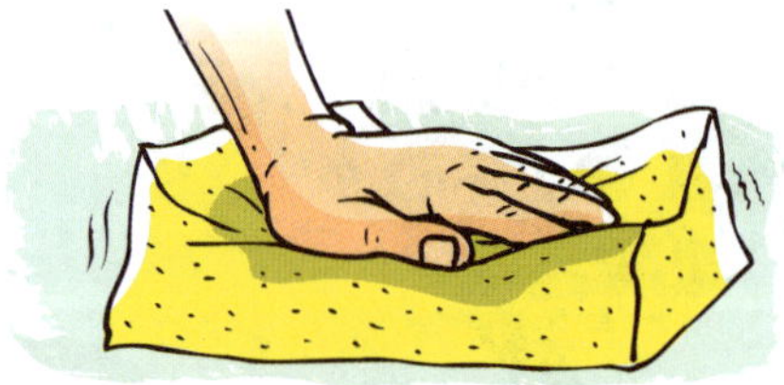

____

3.

____

4.

____

5.

a.

b.

c.

ISBN: 978-1-927042-85-4

B. Label each part of the structure that is either a "strut" or a "tie".

1. Computer Desk

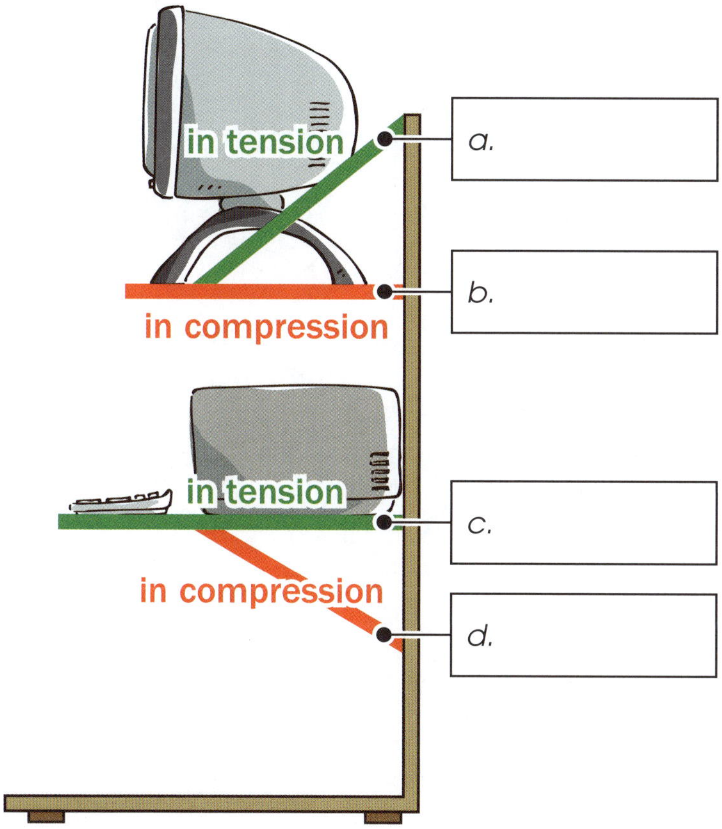

All structures have forces acting on them. The struts in structures are the parts in compression; the ties are the parts in tension.

2. House Roof

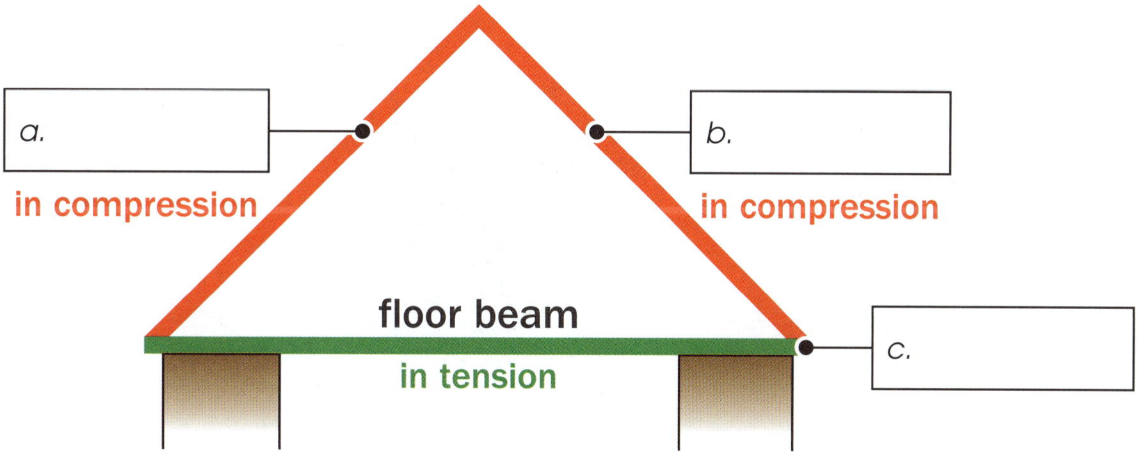

ISBN: 978-1-927042-85-4

C. How do you increase the stability of each of the things below? Colour the correct picture and choose the reason to support your answer. Write the letter in the circle.

- (A) Make some parts of the structure thicker.
- (B) Increase the size of the entire structure.
- (C) Use triangles to strengthen the structure.

1.

2.

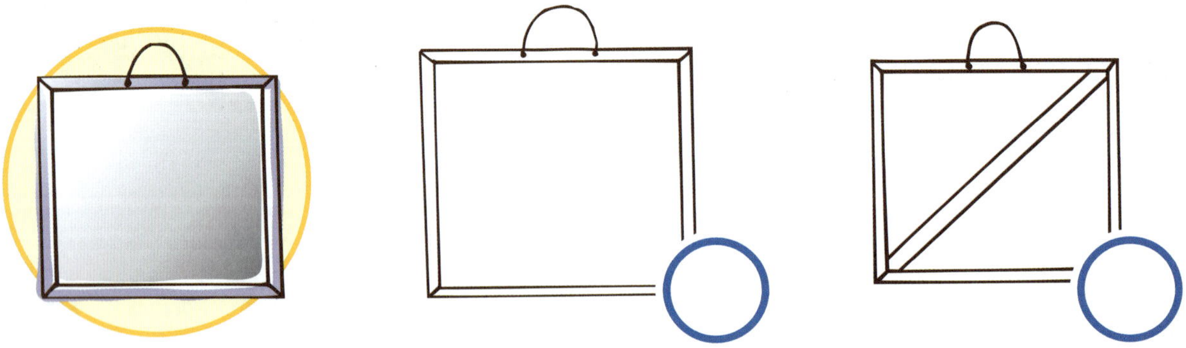

3.

ISBN: 978-1-927042-85-4

D. Fix the structures by redrawing the structures so that they have more strength.

1.

2.

3.

ISBN: 978-1-927042-85-4

8

Try this!

The Strength and Stability of Structures

Materials:

- tape
- weights
- cardboard
- several sheets of paper

You can construct your columns by folding the paper. The cardboard is used as a roof on your column that can hold the weights that you choose.

Record Your Observation

Shape of Column	No. of Weights

1. Which shape of column is the strongest? ______________

2. Which shape of column is the weakest? ______________

Checklist

Are you able to...

- [ ] use different words to describe the effects of the forces at work?
- [ ] identify the struts and ties in structures?
- [ ] use different ways to increase the stability of structures?
- [ ] fix the structures by different ways?

ISBN: 978-1-927042-85-4

Soil

9

In this unit, students will:

- understand that soil is a rich source of life.
- understand how soil is formed.
- understand what composting is and its importance.
- recognize the animals living in soil.

ISBN: 978-1-927042-85-4

9

A. What is soil? Choose the correct words to describe what soil is.

home	mud	sponge
floor	food	ground
cradle	dirt	Earth

Science Corner

Soil is not just dirt but a rich source of life and nourishment for many organisms, including human beings.

The 1. ______________ that soaks up the rain.

A great big 2. ______________ , a natural drain.

The forest 3. ______________ , the 4. ______________ of roots.

The living 5. ______________ beneath our boots.

The speck of 6. ______________ that gets in our eye.

The 7. ______________ in the child's pie.

8. ______________ for animals we rarely see.

Nutritious 9. ______________

for a worm or a tree.

ISBN: 978-1-927042-85-4

B. Read the paragraph and the clues. List the four things that make up soil.

How is soil formed? Over many years, rock is broken down into tiny pieces. Plants and animals die. Their decaying matter and waste called humus joins the broken up rock. Small spaces in the mixture are filled with water and air.

1. It adds moisture.

   ____

2. It cannot be seen, but fills spaces.

   ____

3. It takes many years to break down. ________________

4. It is from the remains of plants and animals. ________________

C. Fill in the blanks with the given words. Then colour the things that may one day become humus.

compost   decaying   nutrients   plants

Humus in soil is good for growing *1.* ________________ because of the *2.* ________________ it contains. In nature, humus is made from *3.* ________________ plants and animal remains. We make humus when we *4.* ________________ .

ISBN: 978-1-927042-85-4

9

D. Read what Jenny says. Answer the questions.

Composting is an excellent way to recycle kitchen waste and garden waste because it helps protect our environment. At the same time, we can use our own composts to improve the soil in our gardens.

Do you know how composting works? Composting is the decomposition of materials originated from animals and plants. These organic materials can be things such as grass trimmings, fallen leaves, eggshells, and tea bags. The composting process produces a dark, crumbly matter that can be used as fertilizer in garden soil. It usually takes 3 to 9 months to complete the whole process.

1. Why is composting important?

____

____

2. How does composting work?

____

____

3. How long does the process of composting take?

____

ISBN: 978-1-927042-85-4

E. **Find and circle the following living things in the word search.**

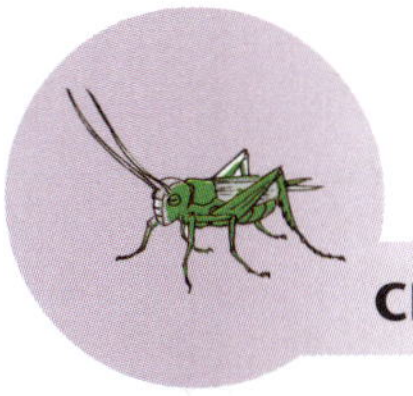
cricket

millipede

ant

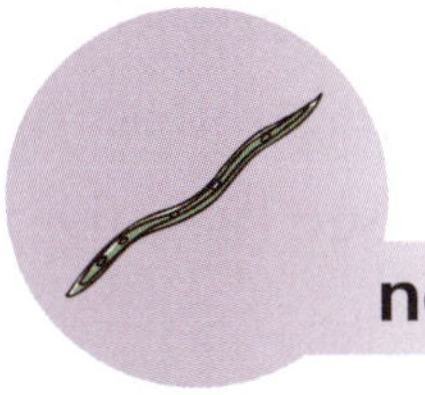
nematode

beetle

snail

mite

earwig

Science Corner

Soil is full of living things. Some, like bacteria and fungi, are too small for our eyes to see unaided. But there are also many other living things that we can see in soil.

t	l	g	s	b	m	i	t	e	z	d	b
y	e	u	n	i	p	a	s	w	b	j	e
r	a	v	a	n	e	m	a	t	o	d	e
u	r	j	i	t	y	e	f	v	b	o	t
p	w	c	l	x	c	s	i	w	t	p	l
m	i	l	l	i	p	e	d	e	y	r	e
n	g	s	e	y	j	g	l	k	w	q	o
b	v	c	r	i	c	k	e	t	a	n	t

ISBN: 978-1-927042-85-4

9

Try this!

Friendly Snails

Snails live in soil. They do not like hot or dry conditions. They like it moist, humid, and shady. They can be found in gardens, in ponds, and even in your backyard. Look for snails early in the morning when dew wets everything. You can collect small snails and put them into a transparent container. Put some leaves in it. Keep it moist and you can observe and see how the snails move.

Don't forget to ask your parents before collecting snails. You can take a magnifying glass with you when you look for snails. It helps you see snails clearly.

Checklist

Are you able to...

- [ ] explain why soil is a rich source of life?
- [ ] tell how soil is formed?
- [ ] tell what composting is and why it is important?
- [ ] recognize the animals living in soil?

ISBN: 978-1-927042-85-4

More about Soil

10

In this unit, students will:

- identify different kinds of soil and recognize their characteristics.
- identify things made of soil.
- learn how rock is broken up in nature.
- understand the importance of preventing soil erosion and find ways to prevent erosion.

ISBN: 978-1-927042-85-4

10

A. Fill in the missing letters to complete the words. Then name the kind of soil you see at each of these different sites.

clay   loam   sand   silt

Kinds of Soil:

1. c________ – It has the smallest rock particles. It is not good for growing plants because water does not drain well and air does not circulate well.
2. s________ – It is often found at the mouth of a river. Rock particles are tiny, but they absorb water well.
3. s________ – This soil has larger rock particles. Water goes through it very quickly.
4. l________ – It has a good balance of three different sizes of rock particles. If the humus content is good, it is the best for growing plants.

5. ________________

6. ________________

7. ________________

8. ________________

ISBN: 978-1-927042-85-4

B. **What is soil being used for in these pictures? Match the words with the pictures.**

- brick house
- beaver dam
- bird's nest
- sandbox
- clay flower pot
- adobe home

1.

Science Corner

People and animals use soil to make shelter and other useful objects. We also make decorative objects and beautiful art with soil as the main material.

2.

3.

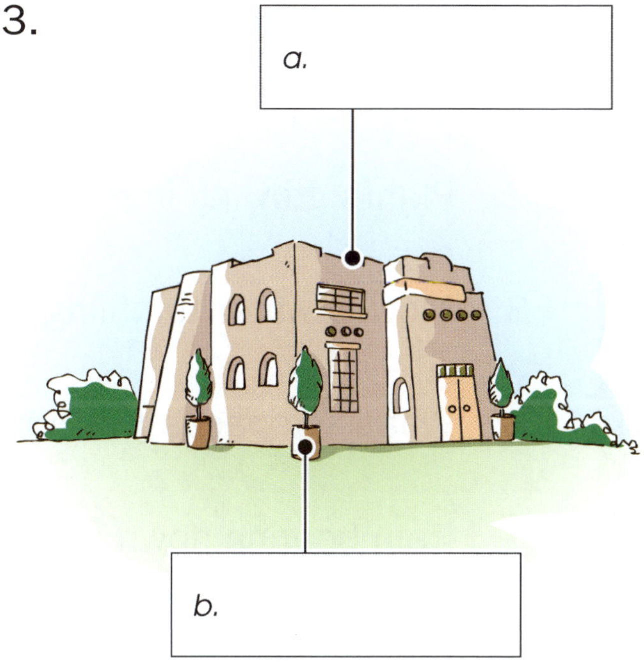

ISBN: 978-1-927042-85-4

10

C. Here are different ways rock is broken up in nature. Match the descriptions with the pictures.

A

B

C

D

E

F

Science Corner

Over thousands of years, rock has been broken up into small pieces by things that happen in the environment. This is called weathering. Rock becomes a part of soil in this way.

1. Wind blowing rock against rock ◯
2. Plants growing in rock crevices ◯
3. Moving water tumbling around rock ◯
4. Water in spaces freezing and expanding ◯
5. Rain beating down and dissolving rock minerals ◯
6. Glacier slowly scraping rock over rock ◯

ISBN: 978-1-927042-85-4

D. Read what Sue says. For each pair of pictures, put a check mark ✔ in the circle to show the one that is preventing erosion from happening.

Erosion is part of nature, but there are things we do that may speed up erosion or make erosion happen. When we do this, we lose valuable topsoil that we need to grow plants. Stop soil erosion! Plants and their roots help keep valuable soil in place. They help soil absorb water.

1.

2.

3.

4.

ISBN: 978-1-927042-85-4

10 Try this!

Soil's Ability to Absorb

Materials:

- cups
- a plastic bottle
- several pieces of filter paper
- different soil samples, such as garden soil, sand, indoor planting soil, and clay soil
- a big container
- water

Remember to use new filter paper for each kind of soil.

Steps:

1. Cut a plastic bottle in half and turn the top half upside down to make a funnel. Then put the filter paper inside the funnel.
2. Fill each cup with one kind of soil and then add water until the cup is full. Let the cups stand for 2 minutes.
3. Pour each cup with soil and water into the funnel right above the big container so that it collects the water drained.

Make a chart to record the results. See which soil absorbs the most water. Use words such as "less" and "a bit".

Kind of Soil	Amount of Water	
	Drained	Absorbed
Garden Soil		

Checklist

Are you able to...

- ☐ identify different kinds of soil and recognize their characteristics?
- ☐ identify things made of soil?
- ☐ explain how rock is broken up in nature?
- ☐ explain the importance of preventing soil erosion and find ways to prevent erosion?

ISBN: 978-1-927042-85-4

A. Complete the crossword puzzle.

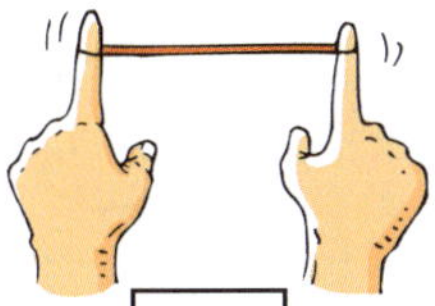

a ________ structure

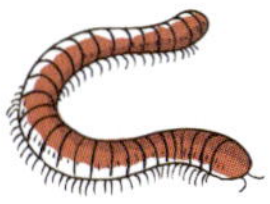

We make humus when we ________ .

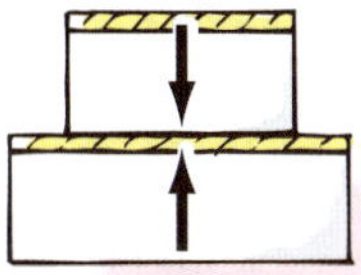

________ forces

This soil has larger rock particles. Water goes through it very quickly.

compost millipede mite

sand balanced stable stretch

ISBN: 978-1-927042-85-4

B. Check ✔ the correct answers.

1. A kind of soil:

(A) silt
(B) loam
(C) clay
(D) beach
(E) copper
(F) sand

2. Animals that live in soil:

(A)

(B)

(C)

(D)

(E)

(F)

3. The device that is controlled by hand:

(A)

(B)

(C)

ISBN: 978-1-927042-85-4

4. Human-made structures:

(A) 

(B) 

(C) 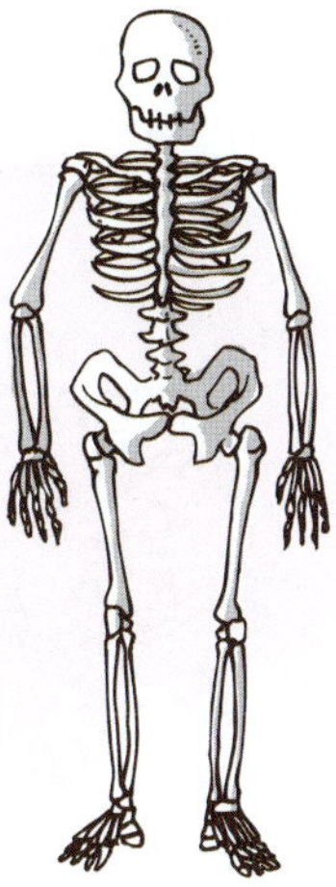

(D) 

(E) 

5. The most stable structure:

(A) 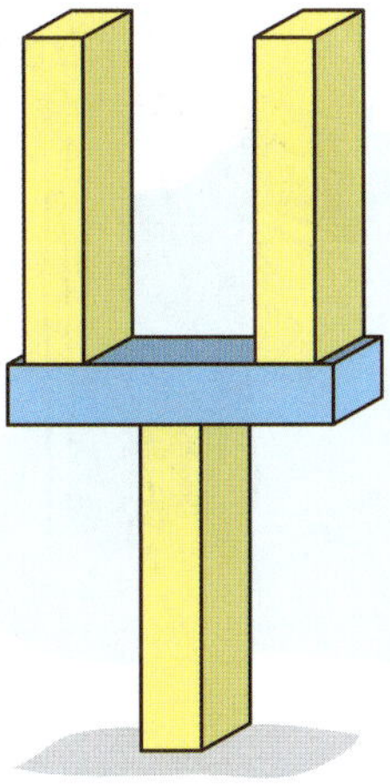

(B) 

(C) 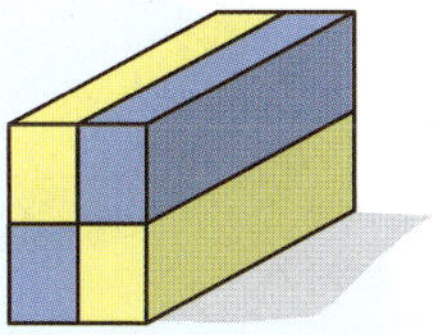

6. The sentence that describes the picture:

(A) the speed and the direction of the ball will be changed.

(B) the ball will travel in the same direction at its original speed.

(C) the speed of the ball will be changed, but the ball will travel in the same direction.

ISBN: 978-1-927042-85-4

C. **Check ✔ the things that are made from plants.**

A

B

C

D

E

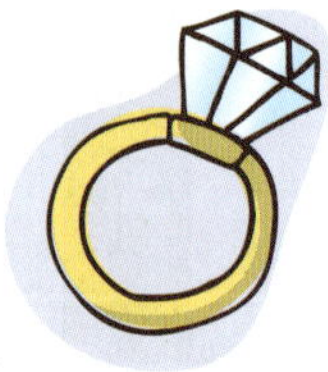

F

G

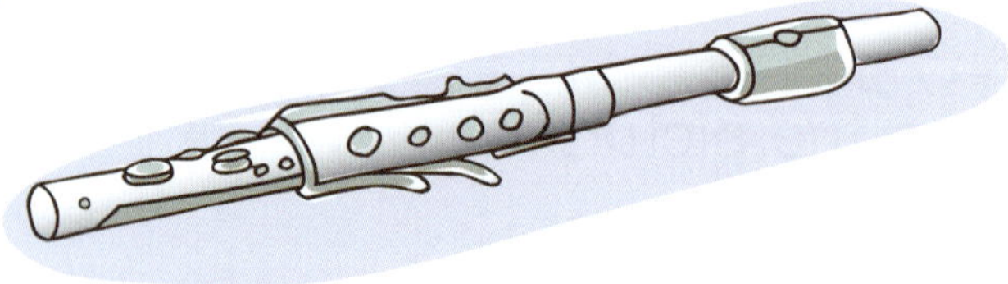

H

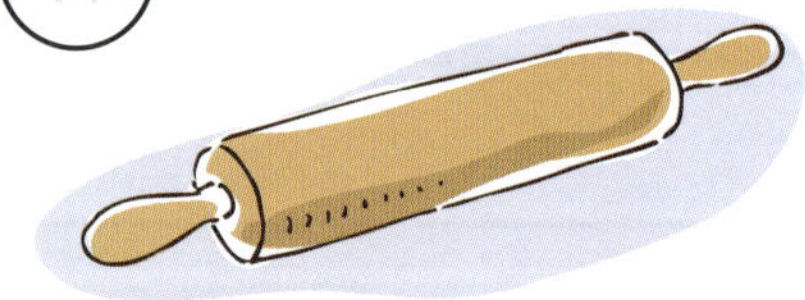

I

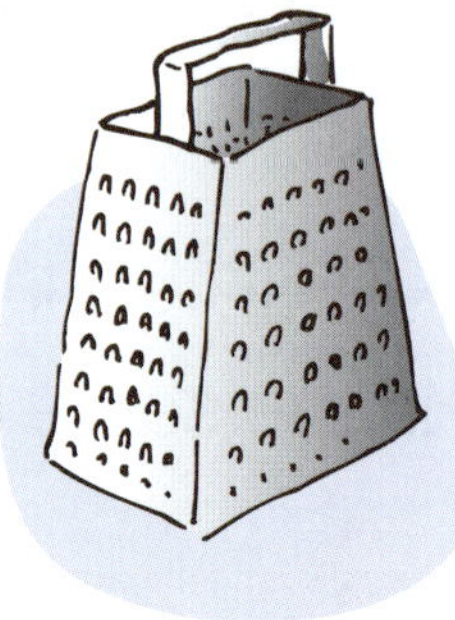

J

ISBN: 978-1-927042-85-4

D. Draw pictures in the boxes to show how you can increase the stability of the structures on the left. Then write sentences to explain your work.

1.

NEW DESIGN

2.

NEW DESIGN

ISBN: 978-1-927042-85-4

E. How much do you know about soil? Take this quiz to test yourself. Put a check mark ✔ in the circle if it is correct.

1. A good soil for your garden ____________ ◯
2. A rock particle, larger than silt ____________ ◯
3. The moisture in soil ____________ ◯
4. The gas in soil ____________ ◯
5. The smallest rock particle ____________ ◯
6. A rock particle, smaller than sand ____________ ◯
7. A mixture of humus, rock, air, and water ____________ ◯
8. Decayed plant and animal remains ____________ ◯
9. It weathers down to smaller particles to become a part of soil. ____________ ◯
10. The breaking down of dead plants and animal matters ____________ ◯

Number of correct answers:

- 7 or more – You are a soil expert.
- Fewer than 7 – You should review units 9 and 10.

ISBN: 978-1-927042-85-4

Answers

ISBN: 978-1-927042-85-4

ANSWERS

1 Plants

A.

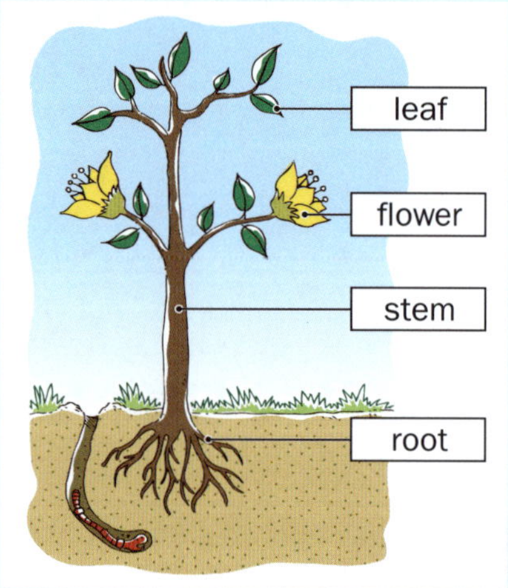

B.

1. 

2. 

3. 

4. 

C.

1. broadleaf ; conifer
2. leaves ; fall ; flowers
3. needle-like ; evergreen

D.

1. sunlight
2. air
3. water

E.

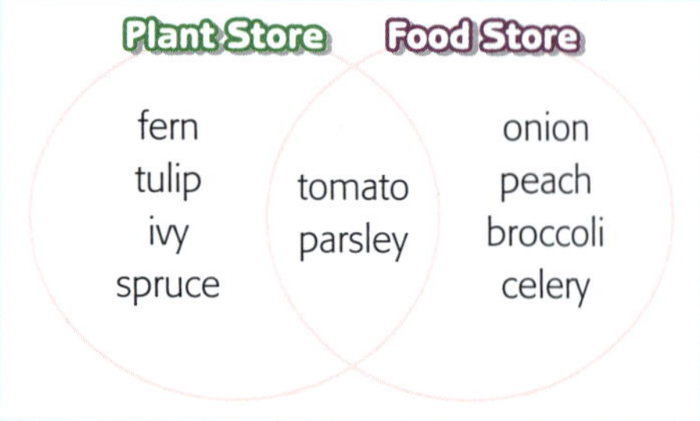

Try this!

(Individual answer)

2 More about Plants

A.

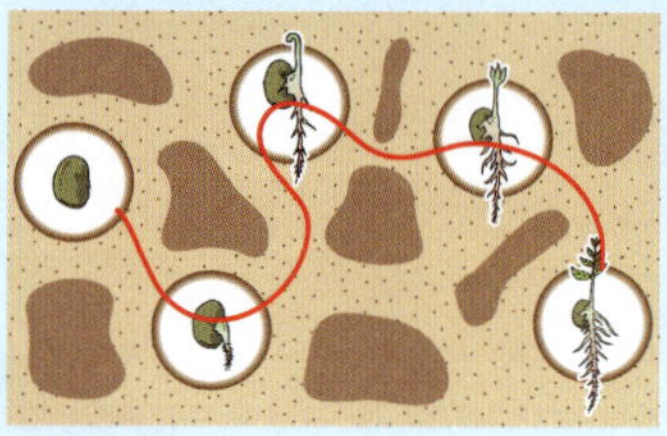

B.

1. winter
2. spring
3. summer
4. fall

C.

1. 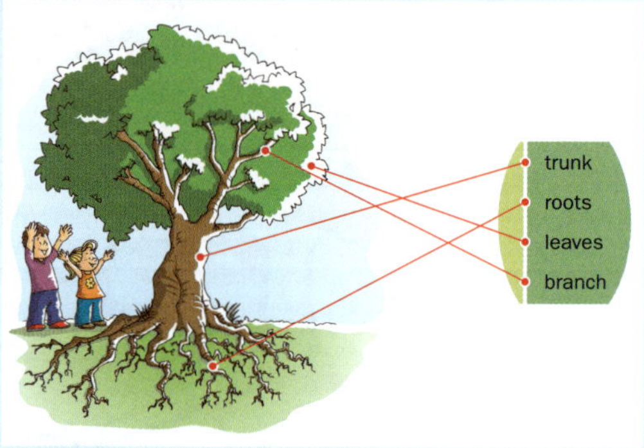

2. plants
3. trunk
4. branches

5-6. water/nutrients

7. leaves
8. bark

D.

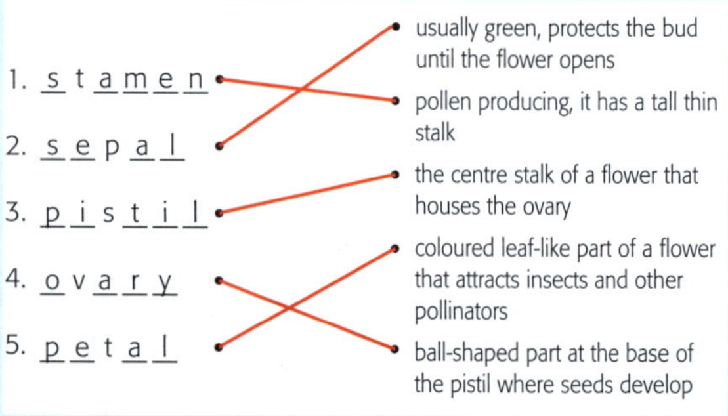

E.

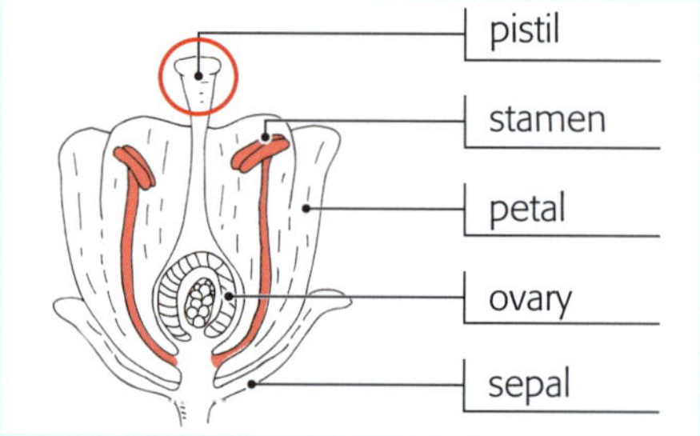

F.

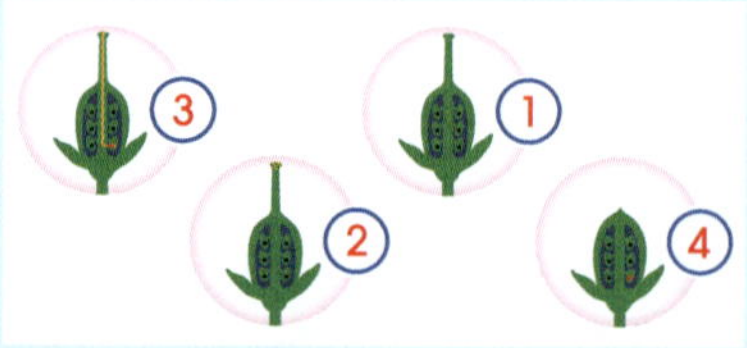

Try this!

(Individual observation)

ISBN: 978-1-927042-85-4

3 Magnets

A. 1. north ; south
2. magnetite
3. nickel ; magnet
4. whales

B.

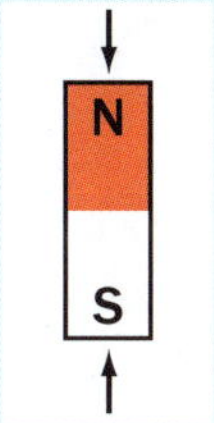

C. 1. south ; Different
2. north ; Like

D. 1. repel
2. attract
3. attract
4. repel

E. 1.

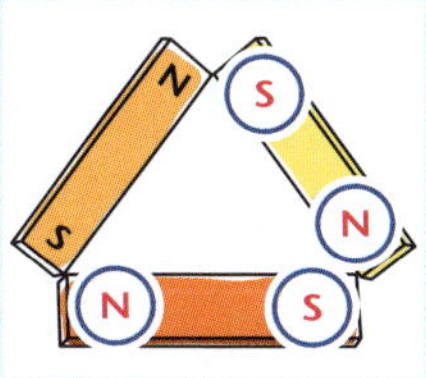

2.

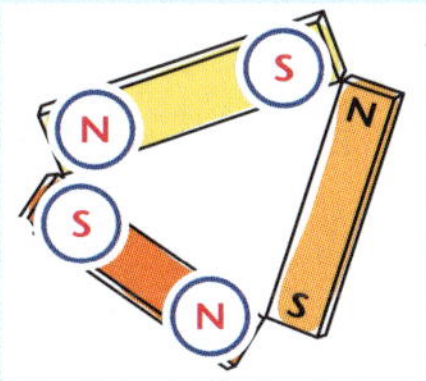

F. 1. magnetite ; north pole
2. iron or nickel ; repel
3. attract

Try this!

(Individual observation)

4 More about Magnets

A. 1. door 2. north
3. stick 4. stripe

B. 1.

2.

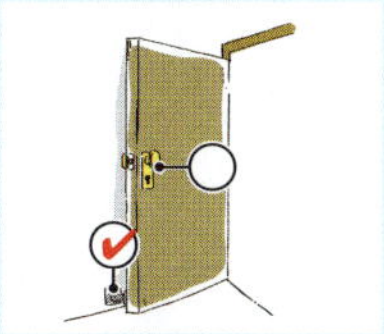

3.

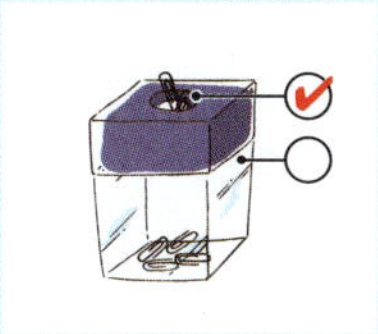

4.

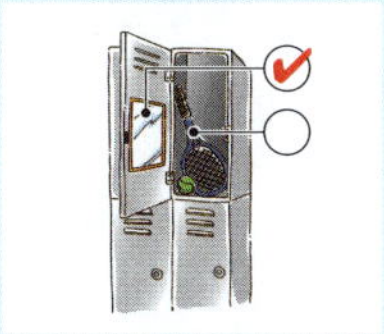

5.

C.

D. 1. It will move forward slowly.
2. It will move forward faster.
3. It will move forward faster than in question 1.
4. The magnet in my hand will attract the magnet on the toy car to move toward it.

Try this!

(Individual observation and answer)

ISBN: 978-1-927042-85-4

ANSWERS

5 Forces and Movement (1)

A. 1. pull 2. pull
3. push 4. push
5. push

B. Colour 1, 2, and 5.

C. 1. Muscular
2. Electrostatic
3. Friction
4. Magnetic
5. Buoyancy
6. Gravity

D. 1. Magnetic Force ; indirectly
2. Electrostatic Force ; indirectly
3. Buoyancy ; directly
4. The Force of Friction ; directly
5. Muscular Force ; directly
6. The Force of Gravity ; indirectly

Try this!

(Individual observation and answer)

Midway Review

A.

						P			
						E			
						T			
				M		A			
	B	R	O	A	D	L	E	A	F
				G					
	M	A	G	N	E	T	I	C	
				E					
				T					
				I					
				T		R			
D	I	F	F	E	R	E	N	T	
						P			
			W	A	T	E	R		
						L			

B. 1. A 2. B
3. B ; C 4. B ; D ; F
5. B ; C 6. B ; D

C. 1. stem 2. roots
3. leaf 4. flower
5. seed

6 Forces and Movement (2)

A. 1. balanced 2. unbalanced
3. balanced 4. unbalanced

B. 1.

2.

3.

4.

5.

C. 1. A 2. B
3. A

D. 1. by hand
2. at a distance
3. automatically
4. at a distance
5. automatically
6. by hand

Try this!

(Suggested answers)
1. Push harder.
2. Stop pushing the cart and pull it toward yourself.
3. The cart will turn.

7 Stability (1)

A. 1. nest ; non-human-made
2. Taj Mahal/a temple ; human-made
3. beaver dam ; non-human-made
4. web ; non-human-made
5. the CN Tower ; human-made
6. hydroelectric dam ; human-made

B. 1. nest
2. the CN Tower
3. hydroelectric dam
4. beaver dam
5. web
6. Taj Mahal/a temple

ISBN: 978-1-927042-85-4

C. 1.

2.

D. 1. A, B, C ; A
2. A, C, B ; B

Try this!
(Individual answer)

8 Stability (2)

A. 1. twist 2. squeeze
3. stretch 4. bend
5a. slide b. stretch
c. squeeze

B. 1a. tie b. strut
c. tie d. strut
2a. strut b. strut
c. tie

C. 1.

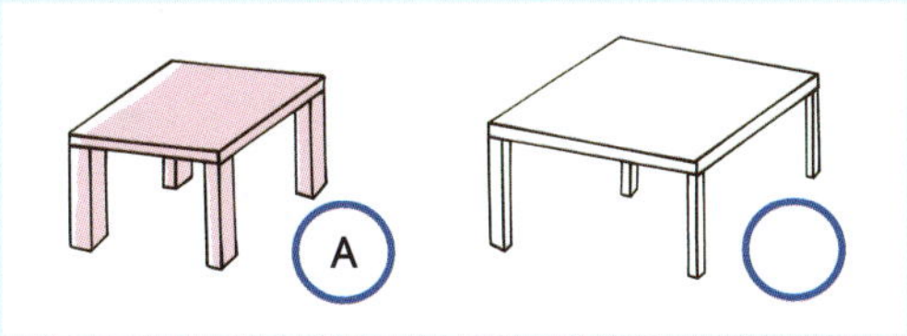

2.

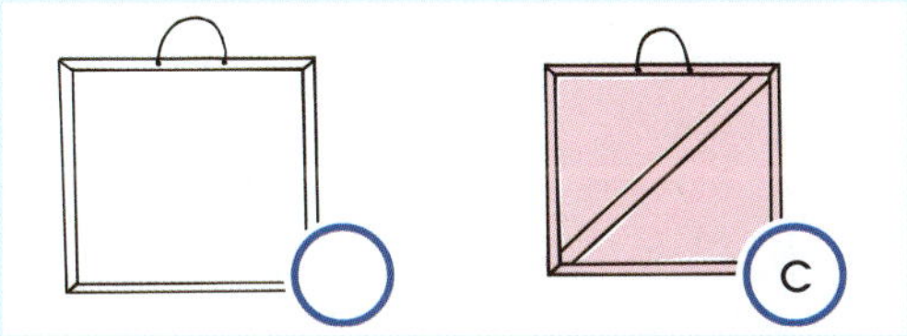

3.

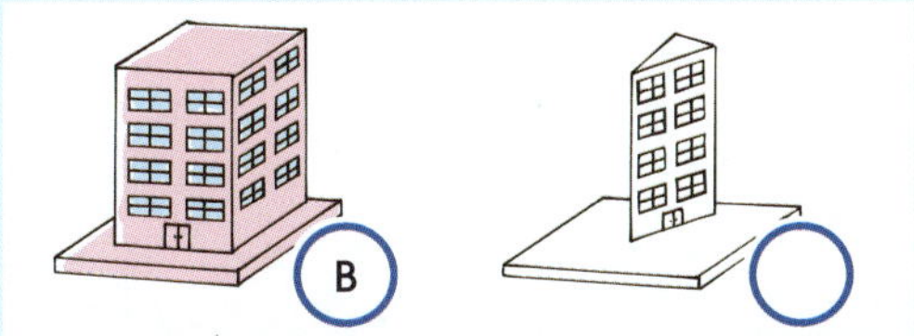

D. (Individual answers)

Try this!
(Individual observation and answers)

9 Soil

A. 1. ground 2. sponge
3. floor 4. cradle
5. Earth 6. dirt
7. mud 8. Home
9. food

B. 1. water 2. air
3. rock 4. humus

C. 1. plants 2. nutrients
3. decaying 4. compost

D. 1. Composting fertilizes the soil. By recycling kitchen waste and garden waste, composting helps protect our environment.
2. Composting produces a dark, crumbly matter from the decomposition of organic materials that can be used as fertilizer in soil.
3. It takes 3 to 9 months.

E.

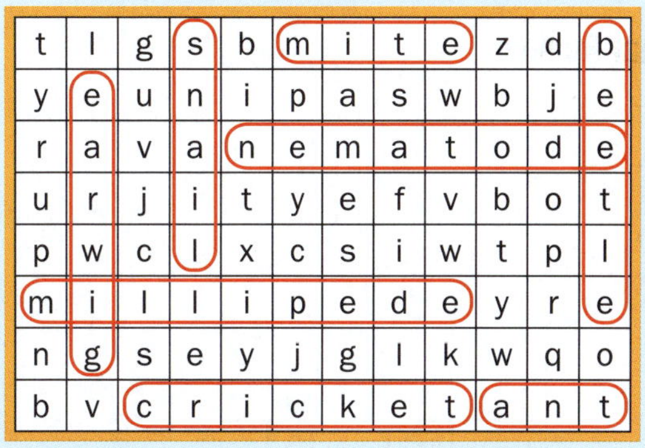

Try this!
Activity

ISBN: 978-1-927042-85-4

ANSWERS

10 More about Soil

A.
1. clay
2. silt
3. sand
4. loam
5. sand
6. clay
7. silt
8. loam

B.
1a. brick house
b. sandbox
2a. bird's nest
b. beaver dam
3a. adobe home
b. clay flower pot

C.
1. B
2. C
3. E
4. A
5. F
6. D

D.
1. 
2. 
3. 
4. 

Try this!

(Individual observation)

Final Review

A.

					M			
					I			
	S				T			
S	T	A	B	L	E			
	R							
	E							
	T							
	C	O	M	P	O	S	T	
	H		I					
			L					
	B	A	L	A	N	C	E	D
			I					
			P					
			E					
S	A	N	D					
			E					

B.
1. A ; B ; C ; F
2. A ; C ; E
3. B
4. B ; D ; E
5. C
6. A

C. A ; C ; D ; F ; H ; J

D. (Individual drawings and answers)

E.
1. loam
2. sand
3. water
4. air
5. clay
6. silt
7. soil
8. humus
9. rock
10. decay

ISBN: 978-1-927042-85-4